LOOK & FIND OUT

Desert Animals

by Alice B. McGinty

Scholastic Inc.

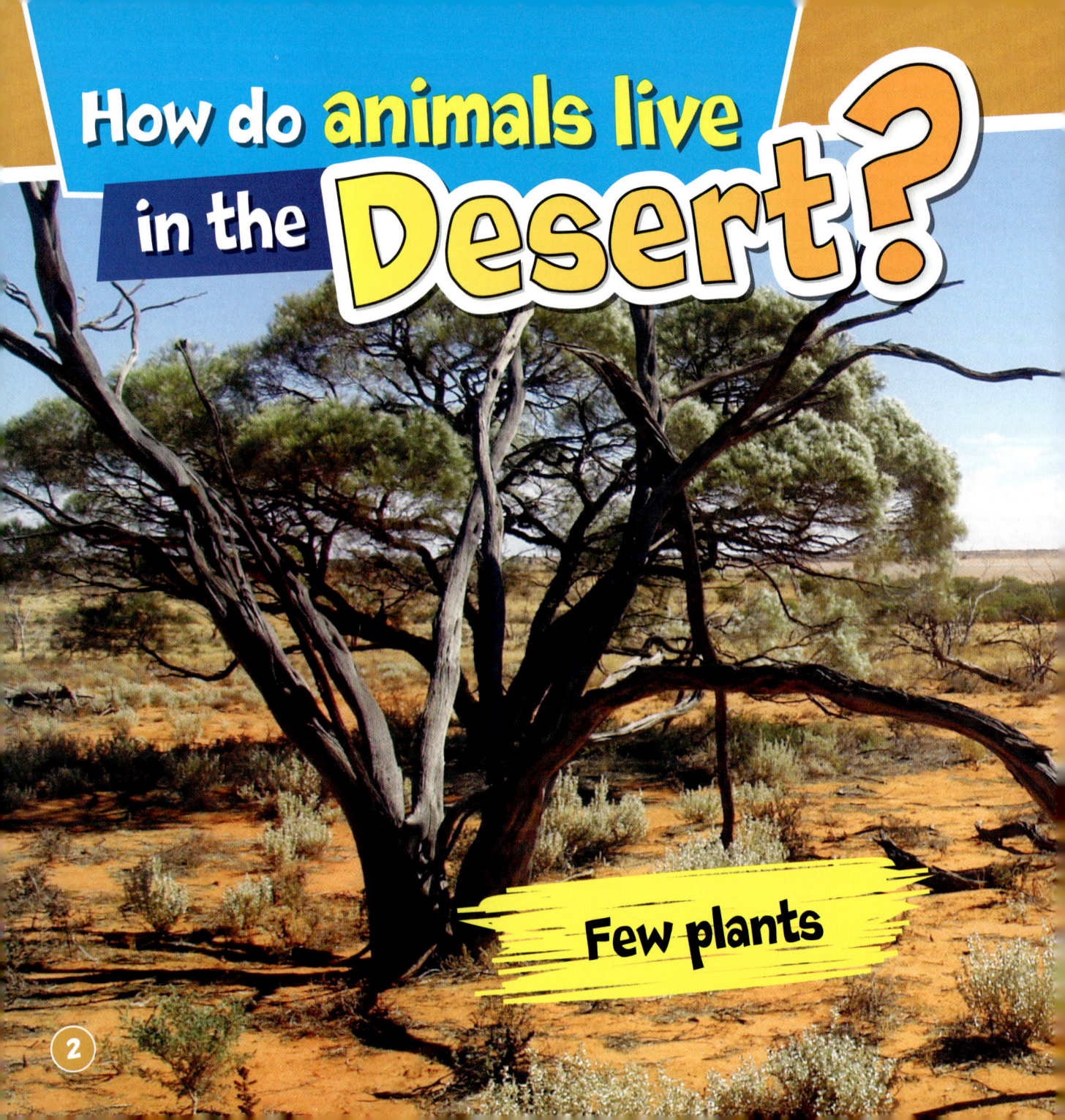

How do animals live in the Desert?

Few plants

Hot in the daytime, cold at night

Little rain

Elf owl

The elf owl nests in holes in desert plants. It sleeps during the hot day. At dusk, the sun sets and the desert cools.

The elf owl comes out to hunt. It flies. It climbs cacti. It catches insects everywhere!

Found in
North America

5

Gila monster

Some animals stay cool by living underground. This Gila monster lives in a burrow.

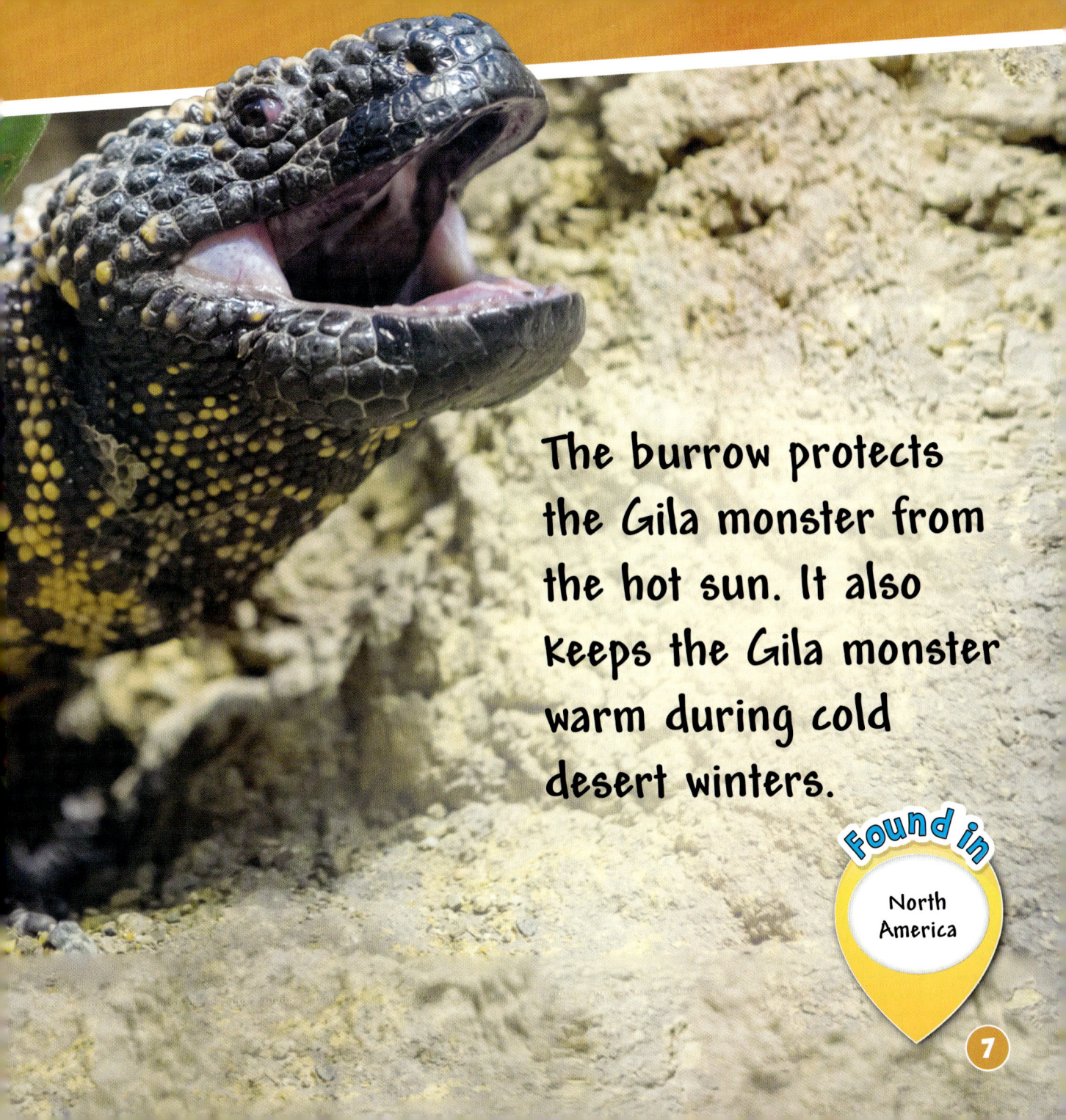

The burrow protects the Gila monster from the hot sun. It also keeps the Gila monster warm during cold desert winters.

Found in
North America

Meerkat

Many desert animals have light-colored coats to reflect the sun. The meerkat's light-colored coat keeps it cool.

Meerkats take turns standing guard, while the others dig for insects. If enemies come, the guard barks a warning!

Found in
Africa

Fennec fox

The fennec fox is the smallest kind of fox. But it has huge ears! Its ears let heat escape from the fox's body.

During cold winters, the fennec fox wraps itself in its bushy tail. Nice and warm!

Found in
Africa

Bactrian camel

Need a drink of water? Not the Bactrian camel. It gets water from the plants it eats. It can go ten months without drinking water.

The Bactrian camel hardly ever sweats. Its body conserves water.

Found in
Asia

Thorny devil

This thorny devil doesn't need to find a water fountain to get a drink.

It can stand in wet sand or under a dew-covered plant. Water travels along its spiny skin to its mouth. The thorny devil opens its jaws. Gulp!

Found in
Australia

15

Find Out More

The elf owl is the smallest owl in the world. It is about the size of a sparrow! When the owl gets hot, it pants and closes its eyes to cool off.

Gila monsters eat eggs and small animals. They store fat inside their big tails. This lets the Gila monster go for months without eating.

Dark circles around the meerkat's eyes block the sun's glare. These natural "sunglasses" help the meerkat spot enemies in bright sun.

The fennec fox's gigantic ears help it stay cool. They hear a lot, too! The fox can hear insects and scorpions digging under the sand.

The Bactrian camel has long, thick eyelashes to keep sand out of its eyes. It can also squeeze its nostrils shut to block the sand.

The thorny devil's gold-and-brown skin changes color to match its surroundings. This makes the thorny devil hard to see!